Contents

STEVEN
FURTICK

NEW YORK TIMES BEST-SELLING AUTHOR OF **GREATER**

SEVEN-MILE
MIRACLE

EXPERIENCE THE LAST WORDS
OF CHRIST AS NEVER BEFORE

MULTNOMAH
BOOKS

SEVEN-MILE MIRACLE PARTICIPANT'S GUIDE

All Scripture quotations are taken from the Holy Bible, New International Version®, NIV®. Copyright © 1973, 1978, 1984 by Biblica Inc.™ Used by permission of Zondervan. All rights reserved worldwide. www.zondervan.com.

All hymn lyrics are in public domain.

Trade Paperback ISBN 978-1-60142-513-3
eBook ISBN 978-1-60142-514-0

Copyright © 2013 by Steven Furtick

Cover design by Ryan Hollingsworth

Published in association with the literary agency of Fedd & Company Inc., P.O. Box 341973, Austin, TX 78734

Published in the United States by Multnomah, an imprint of the Crown Publishing Group, a division of Penguin Random House LLC, New York.

MULTNOMAH® and its mountain colophon are registered trademarks of Penguin Random House LLC.

Printed in the United States of America
2018

10 9

SPECIAL SALES
Most Multnomah books are available at special quantity discounts when purchased in bulk by corporations, organizations, and special-interest groups. Custom imprinting or excerpting can also be done to fit special needs. For information, please e-mail specialmarketscms@penguinrandomhouse.com or call 1-800-603-7051.

Welcome to *Seven-Mile Miracle*

If you've done video studies before, either individually or in a group, you'll probably find this to be unique. For one thing, *Seven-Mile Miracle* is meant to be more than a study. I hope that for you it's a spiritual experience.

Through these seven videos and the pages of this guide, we will walk together on a journey with Jesus Christ. I recorded each of the seven videos on location in Israel. They're based on the seven miles Jesus walked with His disciples on the road to Emmaus in Luke 24.

What we'll experience together are the seven last sayings of Jesus on the cross. I think they will reveal to you the resurrected Son of God like never before—especially in the context of the actual locations where Jesus paid the ultimate price for our sins.

At the end of each video there will be a time of reflection and worship—a song performed on video to provide you with time in the presence of God.

Of course, this video experience is ideal for the weeks leading up to Easter, but it can be used—and *should* be used—throughout the year. Our life in Jesus Christ is founded upon

His work on the Cross, and that indeed is important to us year round.

I encourage you to use this study with your church or ministry, your small group, and also in your own personal time with God. I pray that like the disciples on the road to Emmaus, you will have your eyes opened in a moment, and you will see how God has been with you all along.

Let this be *your* Seven-Mile Miracle.

Steven Furtick

How to Use the Video and Guide for Group and Personal Experiences

This guide and the accompanying DVD are designed to provide both learning and worship experiences. Filmed in the Holy Land on location where the last words of Christ were actually spoken, *Seven-Mile Miracle* will walk you through, individually or in a group setting, the last seven miles that Jesus walked.

Each of the seven sessions includes time for note taking, group discussion, Bible readings, worship, and take-home personal reflections to use during the week.

One of the unique things about this DVD study is the worship time. The end of each video features a worship song. This guide provides direction for using these hymns during a time of personal worship within the group. We encourage you to structure the worship time in a way that best suits your group.

The Personal Reflection segment at the end of each session is intended for personal devotional time during the week that follows, but it can easily be adapted for use within groups.

Likewise, all the group sessions and activities can be used by an individual for private study and devotional time.

Note that the last session includes a time for Communion. Be prepared with the Communion elements, bread and juice, for the group worship.

We pray this will be not only a rich time of learning but also a deep and meaningful personal time of worship.

Session Schedule

INTRO SEVEN-MILE MIRACLE

View the intro video in conjunction
with your Mile One session.

MILE ONE FORGIVENESS

Prayer: "Open our eyes to the full
extent of His forgiveness."

MILE TWO SALVATION

Prayer: "Open our eyes to the
wonder of His salvation."

MILE THREE RELATIONSHIP

Prayer: "Open our eyes to the priority
of our relationship with Him."

MILE FOUR ABANDONMENT

Prayer: "Open our eyes to the
persistence of His presence."

SEVEN-MILE MIRACLE

This study finds us on the Emmaus Road, the very road Jesus walked on the third day after His death on the cross.

In Luke 24, two of Jesus' disciples walked the seven-mile road to Emmaus, discussing what had just transpired on the cross. But it was only after Jesus appeared in the middle of their conversation and after He broke bread with them at the end of their seven-mile journey that they realized who He really was.

The seven-mile journey that the disciples took with Jesus was one of completion and perfection. The disciples had followed Jesus for years, but it was this moment that opened their eyes to see their risen Savior like never before.

As you begin your own journey through the seven last sayings of Jesus, pray that God will open your heart to the work that He wants to do in your life over the next seven weeks or at whatever pace you choose to complete this study.

After you watch the introduction video, go directly into the first session. As you navigate each mile of our journey together, focus your mind and your heart on the teachings you will hear. Take notes throughout, and use the worship time to reflect on the hymns you will hear.

Our prayer is that at the end of this seven-mile journey you, too, will open your eyes to see the risen Jesus like never before.

FORGIVENESS

Father, forgive them, for they do
not know what they are doing.

LUKE 23:34

GOLGOTHA: THE PLACE OF THE SKULL

"Open our eyes to the full extent
of His forgiveness."

TEACHING

Our journey through the seven last sayings of Jesus Christ begins at Golgotha, or "the Skull," widely recognized as the ground where Jesus hung from the cross. It is here that Jesus Christ paid the debt we could never pay, offering His life as an atoning sacrifice for our sins.

Play the video for Mile One. As you watch and listen to Pastor Furtick, follow the selected quotes listed below. Take brief notes in the space provided—whatever comes to your

mind: thoughts, Bible verses, personal experiences, break-through moments.

"Father, forgive them even though they know exactly what they are doing."

The first thing Jesus did was issue forgiveness in the face of His betrayers. Some of them were truly ignorant of the fact that they were crucifying the true Messiah that Israel had been waiting for. However, many of us today know exactly what we ought not to do, but we do it anyway. The miracle of Jesus' forgiveness begins with an inclusive offer of His grace to everyone who has ever sinned against His Father.

_____

_____

_____

_____

_____

_____

"So many times when we sin, it's not a lack of knowledge—it's a lack of passion in our hearts."

Think of those times you have known exactly what God wanted you to do but you didn't do it. Reflect on times you were actively engaged in something you knew was wrong but you did it anyway.

_____

_____

_____

_____

_____

_____

_____

_____

"Forgiveness is setting a prisoner free and
finding out the prisoner was me."

Forgiveness is not only a defensive mechanism based on what
we deserve but an offensive strategy to win the war against bit-
terness in our hearts. Unforgiveness, if ignored, has the poten-
tial to derail destinies and rob you of the person God created
you to be.

_____

_____

_____

_____

_____

_____

_____

_____

"If you don't give it, I don't believe you truly have it."

If you don't forgive, you haven't been forgiven. When you embrace the forgiveness of Jesus Christ, you will flow in the freedom of His Cross. He has forgiven and covered all your sins and is shaping you into a new creation every day—a new creation that freely forgives just as Christ has forgiven you.

GOD'S WORD

Read silently to yourself or have someone in the group read aloud the scene at Golgotha in Luke 23:32–34:

> Two other men, both criminals, were also led out with him to be executed. When they came to the place called the Skull, there they crucified him, along with the criminals—one on his right, the other on his left. Jesus said, "Father, forgive them, for they do not know what they are doing." And they divided up his clothes by casting lots.

For deeper study, read these passages as well:

Matthew 18:21–35
The Parable of the Unmerciful Servant

Luke 16:1–15
The Parable of the Shrewd Manager

Matthew 6:14–15
Forgiving to Be Forgiven

GROUP DISCUSSION

1. As Pastor Furtick stands and speaks at the place of the Skull, what does "being there where Jesus walked" bring to your mind, and what does it cause you to feel?

2. During the video, Pastor Furtick mentioned that there were those about whom Jesus said, "Father, forgive them, for they do not know what they are doing." But there were also those about whom He would say, "Father, forgive them even though they know exactly what they are doing." Which category do you fall under? Why?

3. Scripture makes it clear that Jesus was fully man and fully God. What must He have felt about the circumstances leading up to His crucifixion? Do you think forgiveness was easy for Him?

4. What's the difference between an occasion when you are wronged unintentionally and when you are wronged on purpose? Have you found it possible to forgive that person who wronged you on purpose?

5. Reflect on your notes from the video session. What can you share with the group about your thoughts regarding God's forgiveness of us even though we "know *exactly* what we are doing"?

6. During the video, Pastor Furtick challenged you to think about the times God could have given up on you but forgave you anyway. What changes has God made in your life as a result of His forgiveness? How is God reshaping you right now?

7. Are you offering forgiveness the same way that you have received forgiveness? If not, how can you begin to forgive the way Jesus has forgiven you?

WORSHIP

Nothing But the Blood

What can wash away my sin?
Nothing but the blood of Jesus.
What can make me whole again?
Nothing but the blood of Jesus.

Refrain:

Oh, precious is the flow
That makes me white as snow.
No other fount I know.
Nothing but the blood of Jesus.

Our prayer for Mile One has been for God to open our eyes to the full extent of His forgiveness. During this worship time, pray that God will forgive you for the times you sinned against Him, both knowingly and unknowingly. And pray that those who have never experienced His forgiveness will realize it for the first time during this study.

As you worship, reflect on the following questions:

- What does forgiveness mean to you?
- How can you experience the full extent of God's forgiveness?

- Whom is God calling you to forgive today?

After the song is over, allow the Spirit to lead you in a time of reflection.

Group leader, close with prayer.

PERSONAL REFLECTION

Take some time during this next week to reflect on what God is speaking into your life.

▶ *Scripture: Read 1 Peter 1:1–9.*

Peter, Jesus' most outspoken disciple, wrote this letter as a message of praise and encouragement to the scattered believers of the early Christian church.

Spiritually, you may be in a similar place as these believers. God chose you before you were knit together in your mother's womb, and He has been calling you to acknowledge Him ever since. He has a role for you to play in His kingdom—one that can't be shaken and will never perish. All you have to do is respond.

This is your chance.

Pastor Furtick challenged you to open your eyes to the full extent of God's forgiveness. But this is just the beginning. As Charles Spurgeon, nineteenth-century British pastor and author, wrote, "Even after forgiveness it will require a miracle of grace to recover us from the ill effects of sin."

God's miracle of grace is available to you today, tomorrow, and always. His mercies are made new every morning. As Peter wrote, even though you have not seen Jesus, you can believe in Him, find joy in Him, and receive salvation from Him.

Have you fully embraced the forgiveness that is in front of you today? What has God delivered you from? How has His forgiveness changed you?

Pray: *God, I praise You for delivering me from my past and making me a new creation in Jesus Christ. I pray that You will help me open my eyes to the full extent of Your forgiveness. Give me the vision to follow You as my guide as You continue making me new every day. Amen.*

MILE TWO

SALVATION

I tell you the truth, today you
will be with me in paradise.

LUKE 23:43

VIA DOLOROSA

"Open our eyes to the wonder
of His salvation."

TEACHING

The second marker on our seven-mile journey brings us to the Via Dolorosa, the symbolic route in Jerusalem where many believe Jesus carried His cross. In this video session, Pastor Furtick unfolds for us how the grace Jesus displayed on the cross is God's way of reaching out to us exactly where we are.

Nothing stops the forgiveness of God from flowing into your life except your unwillingness to receive it. Pray that during this session God will open your eyes to see the salvation that is available for you in Jesus Christ.

Play the video for Mile Two. As you watch and listen to Pastor Furtick, follow the selected quotes listed below. Take brief notes in the space provided—whatever comes to your mind: thoughts, Bible verses, personal experiences, breakthrough moments.

"Jesus, remember me when You come into Your kingdom."

The criminals who hung beside Jesus on the cross represented a contrast of the kinds of people Jesus came to save. On one side, a criminal hurled insults at Jesus, mocking Him for not saving Himself. On the other side hung a criminal who acknowledged the fact that he belonged on the cross—but Jesus didn't. His cry was simple but profound: "Jesus, remember me" (Luke 23:42).

_____

_____

_____

_____

_____

_____

_____

_____

"He couldn't save Himself because He didn't come to save Himself."

Jesus had the capability of saving Himself from the torture of the cross. But His death was our only means of salvation. His purpose—our salvation—was bound to the fulfillment of His crucifixion.

_____

_____

_____

_____

_____

_____

"He didn't die for us to be sorry, but so that we can be changed."

Jesus was the last person who deserved to hang on the cross. Each of us belonged in the middle of those two criminals. Jesus didn't—He hung as a result of our sins. But He didn't die for us to pity His fate on the cross. He died for us so that we can be saved through Him.

_____

_____

_____

_____

_____

_____

_____

"A new 24."

When you experience the salvation of Jesus Christ, you become a brand-new creation. Pastor Furtick used the illustration of receiving a new twenty-four-second shot clock in basketball. Through the grace of His salvation, we receive new mercies every single day. Every morning is a fresh opportunity for you to realize the full extent of His salvation.

_____

_____

_____

_____

_____

"Not only should we be saved from our sin, but we should be saved to a holy life."

Too often we forget that our deliverance is not only about being rescued out of our sinful lives, but it's also about being transformed into a new life of freedom, joy, and deep satisfaction in Jesus.

_____

_____

_____

_____

_____

_____

GOD'S WORD

Read silently to yourself or have someone in the group read aloud Luke 23:39–43:

One of the criminals who hung there hurled insults at him: "Aren't you the Christ? Save yourself and us!"

But the other criminal rebuked him. "Don't you fear God," he said, "since you are under the same sentence? We are punished justly, for we are getting what our deeds deserve. But this man has done nothing wrong."

Then he said, "Jesus, remember me when you come into your kingdom."

Jesus answered him, "I tell you the truth, today you will be with me in paradise."

For deeper study, read these passages as well:

Genesis 40:23
Joseph Forgotten

Lamentations 3:19-26
His Mercies Are New Every Morning

Colossians 2:6-7
Continue to Live in Him

GROUP DISCUSSION

1. This video segment was shot on the Via Dolorosa—
   "The Way of Suffering." This is the path Jesus walked
   as He carried His cross. What thoughts does this bring
   to your mind? How does it make you feel to see the
   actual road Jesus took to be crucified?

2. What stood out to you most during Pastor Furtick's
   video? Share your takeaways with the group.

3. How were the perspectives different for the criminals
   who hung next to Jesus, according to Luke 23:39–43?

4. Since Jesus had the power to rescue Himself and the criminals from the cross, why do you believe the criminal asked Jesus simply to remember him?

5. Reflecting on your past, give an example of a moment when you cried out for God to save you from a dire situation. What was His response? What did His response to you reveal about His character?

6. What is your response to knowing that Jesus paid the debt we deserved to pay? What emotion does that evoke in you? How does it inspire you toward change?

7. God's Word tells us that despite the circumstances in our lives, His mercies are new every morning. What makes this meaningful to you? What "new mercies" do you want to experience today?

WORSHIP

The Solid Rock

My hope is built on nothing less
Than Jesus' blood and righteousness.
I dare not trust the sweetest frame
But wholly lean on Jesus' name.

Refrain:

On Christ, the solid Rock, I stand.
All other ground is sinking sand.
All other ground is sinking sand.

When darkness veils His lovely face,
I rest on His unchanging grace.
In every high and stormy gale,
My anchor holds within the veil.

Refrain:

On Christ, the solid Rock, I stand.
All other ground is sinking sand.
All other ground is sinking sand.

Our prayer for Mile Two has been that God would open our
eyes to the wonder of His salvation. During this worship time,

pray for a deeper understanding of what your salvation means: your newfound freedom from your old life trapped in sin, as well as an awareness of what you are saved *to*—what it means to proclaim His salvation to others.

As you worship, reflect on the following questions:

- What does salvation mean to you?
- Describe the new mercies you want to experience today.
- How can you share the perspective of receiving a "new 24"?

After the song is over, allow the Spirit to lead you in a time of reflection.

Group leader, close with prayer.

PERSONAL REFLECTION

Take some time during this next week to reflect on what God is speaking into your life.

▶ *Scripture: Read Romans 5:1–11.*

Jesus died at just the right time.

The apostle Paul wrote Romans primarily as a letter to the unbelievers in Rome. It also serves as one of the most encouraging books in the Bible for any believer in Christ.

In chapter 5, Paul paints a picture of exactly how unreasonable the grace of Jesus Christ may appear by any human standards. Regardless of the sins of your past, you have been justified by your faith in Christ as the resurrected Son of God. And you have the opportunity to rejoice through any sufferings as you await the hope of the glory of God.

Why? Because, as Paul wrote, Jesus died at the exact moment you needed Him the most.

He paid a price that few are willing to pay for anyone. But Jesus extended a hand to you, in the worst of your condition, so you could have an eternal relationship with Him in His death.

How has Jesus reached out to you, even in your lowest state? How will you respond to Him?

Pray: *God, You are the only One worthy of my praise. Thank You for redeeming my life through Your Son, Jesus Christ. I praise You for extending the grace to rescue me at the time I needed You most. And I pray that I will never take my salvation for granted. Let my thoughts, my words, and my actions always reflect my gratitude for the salvation I have received from You, Jesus. Amen.*

RELATIONSHIP

Here is your son...
Here is your mother.

JOHN 19:26-27

THE UPPER ROOM

"Open our eyes to the priority
of our relationship with Him."

TEACHING

The third mile of *Seven-Mile Miracle* brings us to the Upper Room, where Jesus shared the Passover meal with His disciples just before His betrayal. The meal stands as a testament to the depth of Jesus' desire to have a relationship with each of us.

During this next video segment, think about your relationship with God. Pray that He will open your eyes to see the Savior's desire to have an intimate relationship with you.

Play the video for Mile Three. As you watch and listen to Pastor Furtick, follow the selected quotes listed below. Take brief notes in the space provided—whatever comes to your

mind: thoughts, Bible verses, personal experiences, break-through moments.

"How much would your life change if you heard His voice as if He was smiling as He speaks to you?"

If we understood that God is smiling as He speaks to us, that He desires to be in a relationship with us, that He wants us to come into His presence, how much would our lives change?

_____

_____

_____

_____

_____

_____

"The Savior took time to avert His eyes."

In the midst of His agony on the cross, Jesus took the time to acknowledge His mother and His disciple. He knew He would soon be with the Father, but by taking time on the cross to make provision for relationship, He proved His attentiveness to our every need—in every moment.

_____

_____

_____

_____

_____

_____

_____

**"True relationships are not built on rules
to follow."**

Regulations can take you only so far in your walk with Christ.
Jesus didn't die to establish a barrier of rules. He wants a relationship with you—one you can never fully experience by rel-
egating Him to the lawmaker in your life. Open your eyes to
His presence, and embrace the relationship He eagerly desires
with you.

_____

_____

_____

_____

_____

_____

"God has not only saved me; He has favored me."

Jesus didn't die for us simply because He had to. The relationship He desires with each of us is one that He chose. And He

chooses to favor us as we walk with Him. He even says, "I no longer call you servants... Instead, I have called you friends" (John 15:15). There is no contractual obligation in our relationship with Jesus. He has chosen you as His friend.

_____

_____

_____

_____

_____

_____

"See yourself the way God sees you."

Even while He hung in our place on the cross, Jesus looked upon us with favor. Pray that God will reveal the depth of His love for you and allow you to see Him the way He sees you—as His friend. And pray that you will break through any personal barriers that are preventing you from experiencing a true relationship with Jesus Christ.

_____

_____

_____

_____

_____

_____

GOD'S WORD

Read silently to yourself or have someone in the group read aloud John 19:26–27:

> When Jesus saw his mother there, and the disciple
> whom he loved standing nearby, he said to his mother,
> "Dear woman, here is your son," and to the disciple,
> "Here is your mother." From that time on, this disciple
> took her into his home.

For deeper study, read these passages as well:

Luke 22:14–20
The Last Supper

John 15:9–17
Jesus Calls Us Friends

John 14:15–21
Jesus Promises the Holy Spirit

GROUP DISCUSSION

1. Why do you think relationships are important to God? What relationships are important to you?

2. Why do you think Jesus took time to acknowledge His mother and the disciple?

3. Describe your relationship with God. How did you come to know Him? How do you experience Him every day?

4. Some relationships in our lives carry a certain set of rules for us to follow. What are they? Why doesn't Jesus build His relationship with you on a set of rules? Why is Jesus' approach unique?

5. God doesn't love you because He has to. Jesus goes so far as to say He has chosen you as His friend. What does it look like to be a friend of God? How does it change your relationship with Him to know that He looks upon you with favor?

6. Pastor Furtick gave the challenge to see yourself the way God sees you. How does God see you? How does this differ from the way people in the world see you? What does this say about your relationship with Him?

7. What is one area of your relationship with God that you wish to strengthen? Before you continue in this study, what is one way you can commit to strengthening that aspect of your relationship?

WORSHIP

I Have Decided to Follow Jesus

I have decided to follow Jesus.
I have decided to follow Jesus.
I have decided to follow Jesus.
No turning back, no turning back.

Though none go with me, I still will follow.
Though none go with me, I still will follow.
Though none go with me, I still will follow.
No turning back, no turning back.

Our prayer for Mile Three has been to strengthen our relationship with God. During this worship time, spend a few minutes talking with God as a friend. Talk, listen, enjoy Him.

As you worship, reflect on the following questions:

- Why do you think relationships are important to God?
- What does it look like to be a friend of God?
- How can you personally grow in your relationship with God?

After the song is over, allow the Spirit to lead you in a time of reflection.

Group leader, close with prayer.

PERSONAL REFLECTION

Take some time during this next week to reflect on what God is speaking into your life.

▶ *Scripture: Re-read John 15:9–17.*

Jesus calls you friend.

Jesus didn't have to be coerced into having a relationship with you.

John was the disciple whom Jesus called out to on the cross in John 19:27. And here in chapter 15, John wrote that Jesus has chosen us as His friends. Jesus says that He loves us in the same way His Father has loved Him.

What does that mean to you? How are you not just a believer in Jesus but a friend?

If you truly grasp the idea that Jesus wants to have a sincere relationship with you, one in which He gives you all access to God the Father, you will never be the same. All you have to do is love Him.

You will never have to look to God in shame. You will learn to love in ways that you never thought possible. And never again will you ever walk alone. As Matthew Henry wrote in his commentary of John 15, "The joy of the hypocrite is but for a moment, but the joy of those who abide in Christ's love is a continual feast."

Are you ready to call Jesus your friend?

Pray: *God, I praise You for the mercy You have shown me. I thank You for choosing to send Your Son to die for me. Thank You, Jesus, for calling me Your friend. I pray that my relationship with You will never exist out of obligation but out of a sincere desire to know You better. Amen.*

MILE FOUR

ABANDONMENT

My God, my God, why
have you forsaken me?

MATTHEW 27:46

THE GARDEN OF GETHSEMANE

*"Open our eyes to the persistence
of His presence."*

TEACHING

The fourth mile of our journey leads us to the Garden of Gethsemane, where Jesus sweated like drops of blood as He prayed and anguished over the abandonment He would soon experience.

The relationship we have with God through the salvation and forgiveness He grants comes at an immeasurable price—the forsaking of Jesus by His heavenly Father.

Play the video for Mile Four. As you watch and listen to Pastor Furtick, follow the selected quotes listed below. Take brief notes in the space provided—whatever comes to your

mind: thoughts, Bible verses, personal experiences, break-through moments.

"The greatest moment of agony that anyone could ever experience."

In the Garden of Gethsemane, Jesus prayed in anguish as He stared down the coming events that would ultimately take His life. His agony was so great that He sweated like drops of blood as He prayed to have this cup pass from His hands. Jesus, who had lived in perfect union with His Heavenly Father, was about to be separated from His very source of life.

_____

_____

_____

_____

_____

_____

_____

"The anointing of God flows strongest from your life in the times when you are pressed the most."

Gethsemane literally means "olive press." The only way to get oil from an olive is to press it. Jesus was pressed as He faced the abandonment of His Father, but the pressing resulted in an eternal flow of God's grace. Interestingly enough, the Mount of Olives is where Jesus often went to pray to God.

_____

_____

_____

_____

_____

_____

_____

"We may journey seven miles down the road, but He's been with us all along."

Everyone feels abandoned by God in times of despair. But these are moments that God uses to bring us to the point of our salvation. We can't skip these moments, because God wants to reveal to us that He has been with us for our entire journey.

_____

_____

_____

_____

_____

_____

_____

"Jesus was forsaken so that you won't have to be."

Jesus was separated from His Father for a moment so that you would have the opportunity to be with Him forever. He prayed in the garden that He wouldn't have to face the separation from His Father, but He then said, "Nevertheless, not my will, but Your will be done." Jesus endured a moment of abandonment so that you would never again have to believe that you were alone.

_____

_____

_____

_____

_____

_____

_____

GOD'S WORD

Read silently to yourself or have someone in the group read aloud John 14:15–21:

> If you love me, you will obey what I command. And I will ask the Father, and he will give you another Counselor to be with you forever—the Spirit of truth. The world cannot accept him, because it neither sees him nor knows him. But you know him, for he lives with you and will be in you. I will not leave you as orphans; I will come to you. Before long, the world will not see me anymore, but you will see me. Because I live, you also will live. On that day you will realize that I am in my Father, and you are in me, and I am in you. Whoever has my commands and obeys them, he is the one who loves me. He who loves me will be loved by my Father, and I too will love him and show myself to him.

For deeper study, read these passages as well:

Matthew 1:23
God with Us

Revelation 1:8
God Is, Was, and Is to Come

Isaiah 53:1–12
By His Wounds We Are Healed

GROUP DISCUSSION

1. What thoughts and feelings do you have as you watch Pastor Furtick standing and speaking in the actual Garden of Gethsemane?

2. What did you learn from Pastor Furtick's comments in session 4? What stood out to you about the abandonment that Jesus faced?

3. How did Jesus anguish over His calling in the Garden of Gethsemane? Describe a time when you anguished over a decision (big or small) in your life.

4. How did Jesus actually experience abandonment in Matthew 27:46? What makes this the greatest agony that anyone could experience? What makes Jesus' statement in the garden, "Yet not my will, but yours be done," so significant?

5. What is your response to the statement, "Jesus was forsaken so that you wouldn't have to be"? What does Jesus' abandonment teach you about forgiveness?

6. Have you ever experienced abandonment? Personally, what did that feel like? How did this make you feel toward God?

7. Pastor Furtick said, "The only way to get the anointing of God to flow from a life is to press it." What blessings has God brought about in your life as a result of your pressing moments of abandonment? How did the pressing prepare you to receive that blessing?

WORSHIP

I Need Thee Every Hour

I need thee every hour,
Most gracious Lord.
No tender voice like Thine
Can peace afford.

Refrain:

I need Thee, O I need Thee.
Every hour I need Thee.
O bless me now, my Savior.
I come to Thee.

I need Thee every hour,
In joy or in pain.
Come quickly and abide,
Or life is vain.

Refrain:

I need Thee, O I need Thee.
Every hour I need Thee.
O bless me now, my Savior.
I come to Thee.

Our prayer for this week has been to open our eyes to the persistence of God's presence. During this worship time, pray that God will open your eyes to see how His momentary abandonment of Jesus at the cross allows for us to live in His presence forever.

As you worship, reflect on the following questions:

- How did Jesus experience the ultimate abandonment?
- What does Jesus' abandonment teach you about forgiveness?
- Describe a time when you experienced abandonment.

After the song is over, allow the Spirit to lead you in a time of reflection.

Group leader, close with prayer.

PERSONAL REFLECTION

Take some time during this next week to reflect on what God is speaking into your life.

▶ *Scripture: Read 2 Corinthians 4:7–12, 16–18.*

The apostle Paul wrote 2 Corinthians 4 as part of a set of practical applications for the early church in Corinth. Particularly, this passage stands as an encouragement to endure the momentary feelings of abandonment those believers may have been facing.

As Paul wrote in verses 8–9, "We are hard pressed on every side, but not crushed; perplexed, but not in despair; persecuted, but not abandoned; struck down, but not destroyed."

When you find the power for your life in the death of Jesus, nothing can destroy you.

There will be moments of anguish. There will be seasons in your life when you feel as if God isn't there. Times of distress will force you to question whether your relationship with God is real at all.

But these troubles are light and momentary in comparison to the eternal glory that is at work within us through Jesus Christ. Do not fixate on the troubles before you. Look beyond to see what God desires to do in and through you.

The journey of your salvation will not be halted by the devil's attempts to crush your spirit. Whatever distress you are facing right now, pray for God to redirect your focus to the eternal hope of what is unseen.

> **Pray:** *Jesus, I thank You for being forsaken so that I wouldn't have to be. I pray that You will help me recognize Your presence in everything I face today. Help me accept my troubles as momentary and look ahead toward the eternal reward that outweighs everything else. Amen.*

DISTRESS

I am thirsty.

JOHN 19:28

MOUNT OF OLIVES

"Open our eyes to the unending
depth of His love."

TEACHING

The fifth saying on the cross is a cry of distress. Jesus revealed the physical desperation of His dying moments on the cross in the words "I am thirsty."

Play the video for Mile Five. As you watch and listen to Pastor Furtick, follow the selected quotes listed below. Take brief notes in the space provided—whatever comes to your mind: thoughts, Bible verses, personal experiences, breakthrough moments.

"There is a spiritual thirst deep within us."

Jesus experienced a distress that went much deeper than physical pain and dehydration. He thirsted on behalf of our spiritual thirst. All of us long for the satisfaction of knowing that our journey carries a purpose. The torture that Jesus endured was a culmination of the depravity that each of us faces in our distress.

_____

_____

_____

_____

_____

_____

_____

_____

_____

"Everywhere Christ walked, He walked on purpose."

Even as Jesus agonized on the cross, He was in control. The bitter wine vinegar that was given to Jesus was a fulfillment of prophecy. Every moment of Jesus' distress was designed to fulfill a purpose that we could never fulfill.

_____

_____

_____

_____

_____

_____

_____

_____

_____

_____

**"We thirst and are unsatisfied because
we drink from the wrong wells."**

We all experience times of deep distress in our lives. But the
reason we never escape the feeling of being unsatisfied is that we
seek to quench our thirst at the wrong wells. None of our human
relationships or accomplishments could ever produce the satisfaction of drinking from the wellspring of life, Jesus Christ.

_____

_____

_____

_____

_____

_____

_____

_____

_____

"In His distress, He released the greatest
anointing in His life."

There is comfort in knowing that even Jesus grew physically
thirsty. Because He was pressed, He released the greatest anointing that could ever be on His life. He has a purpose for the
emptiness and distress that you feel in your life today. It is all
designed to lead you to a well that never runs dry.

_____

_____

_____

_____

_____

_____

_____

GOD'S WORD

Read silently to yourself or have someone in the group read aloud this passage from John 4:1–26:

The Pharisees heard that Jesus was gaining and baptizing more disciples than John, although in fact it was not Jesus who baptized, but his disciples. When the Lord learned of this, he left Judea and went back once more to Galilee.

Now he had to go through Samaria. So he came to a town in Samaria called Sychar, near the plot of ground Jacob had given to his son Joseph. Jacob's well was there, and Jesus, tired as he was from the journey, sat down by the well. It was about the sixth hour.

When a Samaritan woman came to draw water, Jesus said to her, "Will you give me a drink?" (His disciples had gone into the town to buy food.)

The Samaritan woman said to him, "You are a Jew and I am a Samaritan woman. How can you ask me for a drink?" (For Jews do not associate with Samaritans.)

Jesus answered her, "If you knew the gift of God and who it is that asks you for a drink, you would have asked him and he would have given you living water."

"Sir," the woman said, "you have nothing to draw

with and the well is deep. Where can you get this living water? Are you greater than our father Jacob, who gave us the well and drank from it himself, as did also his sons and his flocks and herds?"

Jesus answered, "Everyone who drinks this water will be thirsty again, but whoever drinks the water I give him will never thirst. Indeed, the water I give him will become in him a spring of water welling up to eternal life."

The woman said to him, "Sir, give me this water so that I won't get thirsty and have to keep coming here to draw water."

He told her, "Go, call your husband and come back."

"I have no husband," she replied.

Jesus said to her, "You are right when you say you have no husband. The fact is, you have had five husbands, and the man you now have is not your husband. What you have just said is quite true."

"Sir," the woman said, "I can see that you are a prophet. Our fathers worshiped on this mountain, but you Jews claim that the place where we must worship is in Jerusalem."

Jesus declared, "Believe me, woman, a time is coming when you will worship the Father neither on this mountain nor in Jerusalem. You Samaritans worship what you do not know; we worship what we do know, for salvation is from the Jews. Yet a time is coming and has now come when the true worshipers will worship the Father in spirit and truth, for they are the kind of worshipers the Father seeks. God is spirit, and his worshipers must worship in spirit and in truth."

The woman said, "I know that Messiah" (called Christ) "is coming. When he comes, he will explain everything to us."

Then Jesus declared, "I who speak to you am he."

For deeper study, read these passages as well:

Isaiah 55:1–2

Come, You Who Are Thirsty

Psalm 69:21

David's Prophecy of Jesus' Thirst

Mark 8:31

Jesus Predicts His Death

GROUP DISCUSSION

1. As a group, share any new takeaways you had from Pastor Furtick's video.

2. Describe the distress Jesus experienced in John 19:28. How was it more than just a physical need? What does this say about the spiritual thirst that exists all around us?

3. What is so significant about the soldiers extending a sponge of wine vinegar to Jesus' lips? What does this show about Jesus' character? How was Jesus still in control in that moment?

4. What kind of distress have you experienced in your life? What "wells" do you typically go to for relief from your distress?

5. Why do you believe that most of our attempts to find satisfaction are unfulfilling? How have you experienced the "wrong wells" in your own life? How did you realize you were drawing from the wrong well?

6. How does God use your distress to lead you closer to Him? What does it mean to drink from the well that never runs dry? How does this change your perspective on facing distress and adversity?

7. What is one well in your life right now that is unsatis-
   fying? What can you do this week to leave it behind?
   What can you do this week to replace it with your
   trust in Jesus Christ?

WORSHIP

It Is Well with My Soul

When peace like a river attendeth my way,
When sorrows like sea billows roll,
Whatever my lot, Thou has taught me to say,
"It is well, it is well with my soul."

Refrain:

It is well with my soul.
It is well, it is well with my soul.

My sin—O the bliss of this glorious thought—
My sin, not in part but the whole,
Is nailed to the cross, and I bear it no more.
Praise the Lord, praise the Lord, O my soul.

Refrain:

It is well with my soul.
It is well, it is well with my soul.

Our prayer for Mile Five has been to open our eyes to the unending depth of God's love. As you worship, pray for a greater perspective on the price Jesus paid to show His love for you.

During this worship time, reflect on the following questions:

- What kind of distress did Jesus experience?
- What kind of distress are you experiencing in your life right now?
- How can you find the right wells to begin drinking from today?

After the song is over, allow the Spirit to lead you in a time of reflection.

Group leader, close with prayer.

PERSONAL REFLECTION

Take some time during this next week to reflect on what God is speaking into your life.

▶ *Scripture: Read Hebrews 12:1–3.*

Written primarily to skeptical Jews, the book of Hebrews builds upon the foundation that is laid in the Old Testament to display how Jesus is the perfection of the Law of the Old Covenant.

It all culminates in the opening of Hebrews 12, where Jesus establishes Himself as the completion of everything Abraham, David, and others were promised but never saw.

This passage encourages us to run the race that God has set out for us. To live out the calling He has uniquely placed on each of our lives.

But you will never finish the race until you fix your eyes on Jesus. He is the one sitting at the right hand of God. He is the author and perfecter of your faith. Not only did He save you from your times of distress, but He is giving you victory over everything you face as you grow into the person He created you to be.

Interestingly enough, this is also the only passage in the Bible that says Jesus actively went to the cross. He didn't just let it happen to Him; He considered it a joy to endure the cross just for you.

You have allowed Him to save you. Now will you allow Him to shape you on your journey with Him?

Pray: *Jesus, thank You for enduring the cross. I praise You for considering it joy to die on my behalf. I pray that I will never grow weary by taking my life into my own hands, but that I will obey You by always looking to You as the author and perfecter of my faith. Amen.*

TRIUMPH

It is finished.

JOHN 19:30

THE EMPTY TOMB

"Open our eyes to the
victory of surrender."

TEACHING

The sixth mile of our journey places us in front of the empty tomb following Jesus' resurrection. When Jesus said, "It is finished," He gave up His life. But in doing so, He gave us access to the eternal victory He had accomplished over Satan.

During this video session, Pastor Furtick stands in front of the tomb believed to be where Jesus was laid. He challenges us not to mourn over the loss of Jesus' life, but to find the power in His triumph over death.

Play the video for Mile Six. As you watch and listen to Pastor Furtick, follow the selected quotes listed below. Take brief notes in the space provided—whatever comes to your mind:

thoughts, Bible verses, personal experiences, breakthrough moments.

"The greatest sabotage in the history of mankind."

"It is finished" is an expression of the brilliance of God. The great story of Creation, the fall of man, and the redemption of mankind culminates in those three words. Despite all the efforts of evil, the frailty of men and women, and the despair of life, God engineered the most extraordinary triumph of all.

_____

_____

_____

_____

_____

"The salvation of God can only begin when your human striving ends."

In human terms, triumph is the culmination of our strength and persistence. But on the cross, Jesus achieved triumph in a moment that none of our efforts could ever replicate. When Jesus said, "It is finished," the devil must have thought there was nothing else Jesus could do. Instead, Jesus was saying that nothing else needed to be done.

_____

_____

_____

_____

_____

_____

"Christianity is not spelled d-o or d-o-n-'-t. It is spelled d-o-n-e."

Our human nature tells us to focus on everything we can or can't do to win the approval of others. But with His dying words, Jesus tells us that work is already finished. God's grace has nothing to do with anything we have done or could ever do. It has everything to do with what was done for us on the cross.

_____

_____

_____

_____

_____

"Jesus didn't die so that we would pity Him."

Jesus didn't endure the anguish of the cross for us to pity Him. He didn't want us to weep over the loss of His life. Instead, He wanted us to establish power in our lives through His death. Jesus has done all that He could do for us with His life. And by giving our lives back to Him in response, we find the power and purpose He wishes to freely give to us.

_____

_____

_____

_____

_____

_____

_____

"There is a purpose in your pain."

Your struggle with sin will not be finished until you see Jesus face to face in Heaven. But Jesus' death stands as an assurance that there will always be a purpose for your pain. God is always working everything in your life for your good. Surrender the pain in your life to His greater purpose, and you will find the victory He has already won for you.

_____

_____

_____

_____

_____

_____

_____

GOD'S WORD

Read silently to yourself or have someone in the group read aloud Luke 24:1–12:

On the first day of the week, very early in the morning, the women took the spices they had prepared and went to the tomb. They found the stone rolled away from the tomb, but when they entered, they did not find the body of the Lord Jesus. While they were wondering about this, suddenly two men in clothes that gleamed like lightning stood beside them. In their fright the women bowed down with their faces to the ground, but the men said to them, "Why do you look for the living among the dead? He is not here; he has risen! Remember how he told you, while he was still with you in Galilee: 'The Son of Man must be delivered into the hands of sinful men, be crucified and on the third day be raised again.' " Then they remembered his words.

When they came back from the tomb, they told all these things to the Eleven and to all the others. It was Mary Magdalene, Joanna, Mary the mother of James, and the others with them who told this to the apostles. But they did not believe the women, because their words seemed to them like nonsense. Peter, however, got up and ran to the tomb. Bending over, he saw the strips of linen lying by themselves, and he went away, wondering to himself what had happened.

For deeper study, read these passages as well:

Matthew 28:1–10

The Resurrection

1 Corinthians 15:50–57

Victory Through Jesus

1 John 5:1–5

Jesus Overcomes the World

GROUP DISCUSSION

1. How does it affect you personally and emotionally to see the location where it is believed Jesus rose from the grave?

2. When Jesus said, "It is finished," at first glance, how did this announce a victory over the devil?

3. What does Pastor Furtick mean when he speaks of the resurrection as the "greatest sabotage in history"?

4. Pastor Furtick said, "The salvation of God can only begin where your human striving ends." What does it look like to attempt to earn your salvation? Why is this effort such a common practice?

5. Pastor Furtick also said, "Christianity is not spelled d-o or d-o-n-'-t. It is spelled d-o-n-e. " What does this mean in your life?

6. Jesus didn't die on the cross for you to pity Him. He wanted to establish power in your life through His death. How do you push through the feelings of shame and condemnation and embrace life change?

7. How has God used pain in your past for a greater purpose? What pain are you going through right now? How can God use it for His glory?

WORSHIP

Christ, the Lord, Is Risen Today

Christ, the Lord, is risen today. Alleluia!
Sons of men and angels say, Alleluia!
Raise your joys and triumphs high. Alleluia!
Sing, ye heavens, and earth reply, Alleluia!

Vain the stone, the watch, the sea. Alleluia!
Christ hath burst the gates of hell. Alleluia!
Death in vain forbids His rise. Alleluia!
Christ hath opened paradise. Alleluia!

Our prayer for Mile Six has been to open our eyes to the victory of surrender. As you worship, focus your heart on the act of surrender—how Jesus surrendered His life and how you surrender your life back to Him. During this worship time, reflect on the following questions:

- What did Jesus mean by saying, "It is finished"?
- How has God used pain in your life to help you?
- How can you learn to walk in the triumph of the Cross?

After the song is over, allow the Spirit to lead you in a time of reflection.

Group leader, close with prayer.

PERSONAL REFLECTION

Take some time during this next week to reflect on what God is speaking into your life.

▶ *Scripture: Read Romans 8:28–39*

Very few passages in the Bible claim the triumph of the Cross as Paul does in Romans 8. Let this particular passage stand as one that you can always turn to in times of triumph or distress.

You've traveled six miles on your *Seven-Mile Miracle* journey. You've experienced the forgiveness and salvation of Jesus Christ. But you've also felt the moments of abandonment and distress that have plagued your relationship with Him.

Today take refuge in the fact that none of it is wasted. God is working all things for the good of those who love Him.

But what happens next? What if you don't know how to respond to the resistance the devil has in store for your future?

Paul wrote in verses 36–39 that we are subject to these attacks all day long. But nothing—no matter what circumstances may tell you—can ever separate you from the love of God that is in Jesus Christ.

Take a look at the circumstances in your life today. What is left to hold you back from the victory that ultimately awaits you? How will you find the strength to overcome it?

> **Pray:** *God, thank You for having a purpose for my pain. Your Word says that You will work all things for my good and nothing can separate me from Your love. I pray that whatever I face today, I will praise You for using it to bring me closer to You. Amen.*

REUNION

Father, into your hands
I commit my spirit.

LUKE 23:46

EMMAUS

"Open our eyes to see the
resurrected Son of God."

TEACHING

Our journey together concludes with the seventh mile. In Luke 24, it wasn't until the disciples had reached their destination and broken bread with Jesus that they recognized Him for who He truly was.

The final video of the *Seven-Mile Miracle* series will give you the opportunity to open your eyes in the same way that the disciples opened theirs. Pastor Furtick will lead you through a short teaching and give your group the opportunity to partake in Communion together.

Play the video for Mile Seven. As you watch and listen to Pastor Furtick, follow the selected quotes listed below. Take brief notes in the space provided—whatever comes to your mind: thoughts, Bible verses, personal experiences, breakthrough moments.

"What was it in the breaking of the bread that caused the disciples to see Jesus?"

They saw something in the way Jesus broke the bread that caused them to see who Jesus was. Was it in the movement of His hands, the sound of His voice, or in the simple act of sharing the meal that they recognized Him?

_____

_____

_____

_____

_____

"The Resurrection is not an event. It is a person."

This journey was not designed for you to recall an event. It was designed for you to see the Savior. Jesus was not just resurrected; He is the Resurrection. Just as the disciples' hearts burned within them on their journey to Emmaus, the death and resurrection of Jesus Christ is meant to stir within you a recognition of who He is.

_____

_____

_____

_____

_____

_____

"He took the bread, blessed it, broke it, and gave it to them."

Despite walking alongside Jesus for seven miles, His own disciples did not recognize Him until He broke bread with them at the end of the journey. The breaking of the bread is symbolic of the way God uses us—He takes us, blesses us, breaks us, and gives us to the world. Pray that whatever stage you are in, when you realize that you have been with Jesus all along, you will be able to see the purpose God has for you.

_____

_____

_____

_____

_____

"They saw the nail-scarred hands of the Son of God."

As the disciples experienced, the circumstances of life can blind you from seeing God in your life, even if He walks right alongside you. But when Jesus broke bread with His disciples and gave the bread to them, they saw the nail-scarred hands that were reaching out to them. Pray that Jesus will be revealed to you as He gives His life for you.

_____

_____

_____

_____

_____

_____

"The seventh mile—a mile of completion."

There is significance behind Jesus revealing Himself at the end of the seventh mile. It is seen as a mile of completion and perfection. So as you conclude the journey of the *Seven-Mile Miracle,* pray that you will be reunited with God in a new way. As you partake in Communion, thank God for offering completion and perfection through His Son.

_____

_____

_____

_____

_____

_____

GOD'S WORD

Read silently to yourself or have someone in the group read aloud Luke 24:30–35:

> When he was at the table with them, he took bread, gave thanks, broke it and began to give it to them. Then their eyes were opened and they recognized him, and he disappeared from their sight. They asked each other, "Were not our hearts burning within us while he talked with us on the road and opened the Scriptures to us?"
>
> They got up and returned at once to Jerusalem. There they found the Eleven and those with them, assembled together and saying, "It is true! The Lord has risen and has appeared to Simon." Then the two told what had happened on the way, and how Jesus was recognized by them when he broke the bread.

For deeper study, read these passages as well:

John 11:25–26
Jesus Is the Resurrection and the Life

Matthew 14:13–21
Jesus Feeds the Five Thousand

Genesis 22:1–19
God Tests Abraham

GROUP DISCUSSION

1. How was Jesus reunited with His Father in Luke 23:46?

2. In the video Pastor Furtick said, "The Resurrection isn't an event; it's a person." How does this change your perception of Jesus' resurrection?

3. How did Jesus reveal Himself to His disciples in Luke 24:30–35? Why do you believe that He waited until He broke bread with them after the seventh mile to do so?

4. How have you personally *recognized* Jesus in your life? At what point would you consider yourself "reunited" with Him?

5. In your own words, describe the pattern of God taking, blessing, and breaking His chosen people. How has Jesus taken, blessed, and broken your life?

6. Just as He did with Jesus, God breaks us for a purpose. What purpose do you believe God has for the breaking stages of your life?

7. As we complete the seventh mile together, how has Jesus revealed Himself to you in a fresh way? What is one paradigm shift you have experienced over the *Seven-Mile Miracle* journey? This week commit to sharing this shift with someone close to you.

WORSHIP

Blessed Assurance

Blessed assurance, Jesus is mine.
O what a foretaste of glory divine.
Heir of salvation, purchase of God,
Born of His Spirit, washed in His blood.

Refrain:

This is my story; this is my song,
Praising my Savior all the day long.
This is my story; this is my song,
Praising my Savior all the day long.

Perfect submission, all is at rest.
I in my Savior am happy and blessed,
Watching and waiting, looking above,
Filled with His Spirit, lost in His love.

Refrain:

This is my story; this is my song,
Praising my Savior all the day long.
This is my story; this is my song,
Praising my Savior all the day long.

Our prayer for Mile Seven has been to open our eyes to see the resurrected Son of God. How has that happened for you in a special way during this time?

Use this worship time to share Holy Communion together. First pass around the bread and juice. Have each person partake of the elements whenever he or she feels led during the worship song.

As you worship and partake in Communion, reflect on the following questions:

- How does Jesus seek a reunion with you?
- How has Jesus taken, blessed, and broken your life?
- What do you think God is doing to give you to the world?

After the song is over, allow the Spirit to lead you in a time of reflection.

Group leader, close with prayer.

PERSONAL REFLECTION

Take some time during this next week to reflect on what God is speaking into your life.

▶ *Scripture: Read Luke 22:14–20.*

As Jesus prepared for the agonizing fate that awaited Him, He made it a point to sit down and share a meal with His disciples. In verse 15 He says, "I have eagerly desired to eat this Passover with you before I suffer."

God did not send Jesus to die on the cross as an obligatory price to pay for your salvation. Rather, He eagerly desires a relationship with you.

He told His disciples that the time had come for Him to suffer. He asked them to eat the bread, which represented His body, broken for them, and to drink the cup representing His blood, which would be poured out for their salvation.

Each of the seven sessions of this study was designed to show you the life that Jesus offers you through His death. As you conclude the *Seven-Mile Miracle* study, reflect on everything that Jesus has done for you. Thank Him for saving you. Praise Him for the purpose behind your pain. Celebrate the life you are now able to live because of His death.

And thank Him for eagerly desiring to do it all just for you.

Pray: *Jesus, I praise You as the resurrected Son of God. Your Word says that You are the Bread of Life, so as I take this bread today, I pray that I will never lose sight of who You are. You are my Savior and my Source of life. Thank You for dying on the cross so that I may experience an eternal reunion with You. Amen.*

YOUR SEVEN-MILE MIRACLE

In Luke 24 the disciples walked with Jesus for seven miles, but it wasn't until they broke bread with Him that their eyes were opened to recognize Jesus for who He really was.

As you conclude your seven-mile journey, I pray that your eyes have opened to the risen Son of God like never before. I pray that your perspective has shifted toward a greater understanding of who Jesus is, what He has done for you, and how you can follow Him from this day forward.

Consider using this study again throughout the year or at any time you feel God calling you to draw near to Him.

Whether you have known Jesus—or known of Him—your entire life or are just coming to truly know Him for the very first time, let this study stand as the moment that Jesus initiated a transformation in your life.

Let Jesus turn this journey into a lifelong walk devoted to following Him.

May your moment of realization enable Jesus to move in your life like never before.

Find yourself flowing in the grace and forgiveness of Jesus.

And I pray you will be forever changed by the presence of Jesus in your life.

Open your eyes. This is your Seven-Mile Miracle.

Steven Furtick